Creating a Habitat

Saskia Lacey

Smithsonian

Contributing Author

Jennifer Lawson

Consultants

Jennifer Zoon
Communications Specialist
Smithsonian's National Zoo

Sharon Banks
3rd Grade Teacher
Duncan Public Schools

Publishing Credits

Rachelle Cracchiolo, M.S.Ed., *Publisher*
Conni Medina, M.A.Ed., *Managing Editor*
Diana Kenney, M.A.Ed., NBCT, *Content Director*
Véronique Bos, *Creative Director*
Robin Erickson, *Art Director*
Michelle Jovin, M.A., *Associate Editor*
Mindy Duits, *Senior Graphic Designer*
Smithsonian Science Education Center

Image Credits: front cover, p.1, pp.2–3, p.4 (bottom), pp.4–5(all), p.7, p.9, p.10, p.11, p.12, 13 (top), p.15, p.18, p.19, p.20 (bottom), p.22, pp.22–23 (bottom), pp.26–27 (all) © Smithsonian; p.14, p.17 (bottom), p.23 (top) Courtesy blackfootedferret.org; pp.20–21 USFWS Mountain-Prairie; p.21 (bottom) National Park Service; p.24 John Ashley; all other images from iStock and/or Shutterstock.

Library of Congress Cataloging-in-Publication Data
Names: Lacey, Saskia, author.
Title: Creating a habitat / Saskia Lacey.
Description: Huntington Beach, CA : Teacher Created Materials, [2019] | Audience: K to Grade 3. | Includes index. |
Identifiers: LCCN 2018030208 (print) | LCCN 2018034795 (ebook) | ISBN 9781493869039 | ISBN 9781493866632
Subjects: LCSH: Zoo keepers--Juvenile literature. | Zoo animals--Housing--Juvenile literature.
Classification: LCC QL50.5 (ebook) | LCC QL50.5 .L33 2020 (print) | DDC 590.73--dc23
LC record available at https://lccn.loc.gov/2018030208

Smithsonian

© 2019 Smithsonian Institution. The name "Smithsonian" and the Smithsonian logo are registered trademarks owned by the Smithsonian Institution.

Teacher Created Materials

5301 Oceanus Drive
Huntington Beach, CA 92649-1030
www.tcmpub.com
ISBN 978-1-4938-6663-2
© 2019 Teacher Created Materials, Inc.

Table of Contents

New Worlds

Today is special. You are at a zoo, and there is so much to see! There are many creatures. Each **enclosure** is its own world. Each is a **habitat**, or home, for a different animal.

You see a mongoose. It comes out of its tunnel to eat an insect. You see a fox. It naps on a pile of rocks in the sunshine. You also see a rodent. It sits on a large branch in its enclosure.

Yes, today is special. You are at Smithsonian's National Zoo. At the Small Mammal House, you will see wonderful new worlds!

A fennec fox naps at the Small Mammal House.

A dwarf mongoose comes out of its tunnel at the Small Mammal House.

A degu rodent sits on a branch.

A Goeldi's monkey sits on a branch in its enclosure.

The Perfect Fit

Enclosures are made to fit the needs of creatures. For example, a monkey needs a space that fits tall trees. Spaces are also designed with visitors in mind. They have large windows so that people can see inside.

To be happy and healthy, creatures need the right homes. At zoos, enclosures are their homes. They are made with creatures in mind.

When creating a zoo home, designers ask many questions. Should it be hot or cold? What kind of plants should be there? Should it have other creatures? These questions help designers meet animals' needs.

Designers find these answers by looking at creatures' **natural** habitats. Their zoo homes should **mimic** their homes in the wild. This takes time and research. Once that is done, animal keepers have to take care of the creatures.

Two black-footed ferrets come out of a tunnel.

Daily Duties

Caring for creatures is a full-time job. Keepers arrive bright and early. They have many tasks to do.

Feeding

Keepers make meals for each creature. The food they make depends on what the creature eats in the wild. Some animals eat fruits and vegetables. Other animals eat meat. At the zoo, they get those meals too. Keepers want to mimic what each creature eats in the wild.

A creep of tortoises eats vegetables.

A lemur eats fruit.

A black-footed ferret cleans itself after a meal.

A Proper Meal

In one year, one wild ferret can eat over a hundred prairie dogs! Keepers use that information to figure out how much food ferrets need each day. Then, keepers make sure they have the right amount of food to feed all the ferrets at the zoo.

Animal Enrichment

Keepers want to keep their creatures active. So, each habitat has **enrichment**. These are toys that help creatures use the skills and behaviors they need to survive in the wild.

Black-footed ferrets might have a few toy balls. Ferrets can swat at the balls and chase them as if they are hunting. Or, ferrets might have paper bags. The bags make loud, crinkly sounds. These toys teach ferrets to chase things and listen closely. Those are both skills they would use in the wild.

A group of black-footed ferrets chases each other through a tunnel.

A black-footed ferret waits to jump through a tube into its enclosure.

Some ferrets have tubes on the sides of their enclosures. These tubes mimic **burrows** they would have in the wild.

Tracking Creature Health

Keepers also track the health of creatures at their zoos. It is an important part of the job. They watch what creatures eat and how they act. They note how they play with others. Do they play with their toys? Keepers track that too!

All this information helps keepers. They can learn how to keep creatures safe. They can also use it to learn why some creatures do better in the wild. This knowledge can help keep animals from danger. It can even help save **species**!

A keeper rewards a monkey with a strawberry after checking his health.

A veterinarian checks a newborn fishing cat's eyes.

Poop Sleuth

There are scientists who only work with animal poop! They test poop to look for certain chemicals. These chemicals teach scientists a lot. Scientists can find out whether an animal is healthy. They can also find out whether an animal is pregnant.

13

Meet the Black-Footed Ferret

While at the Small Mammal House, you will see many animals. Some are in zoos because they are being hunted in the wild. Other animals are in zoos because they do not have enough food in the wild. That is the case for one animal in the Small Mammal House—the black-footed ferret.

Black-footed ferrets have a lot of energy. Young ferrets wrestle each other. They are fun to watch. In the wild, they are in danger. But in zoos, keepers study ferrets' behaviors. They can keep ferrets safe.

Black-footed ferrets come out of their burrow at dusk.

Ferrets "talk" to each other. They hiss when they are scared and chatter to warn other ferrets.

prairie dog

flea

At Risk

Black-footed ferrets mainly eat prairie dogs. Prairie dogs are a type of squirrel. They dig burrows, or underground tunnels. Ferrets live in those same tunnels.

Ferrets need prairie dogs to survive. They provide both food and shelter for ferrets. Years ago, a disease spread from fleas to prairie dogs. It killed many of them. It killed some ferrets too. Soon, the ferrets that were left did not have enough to eat. Many more ferrets died from hunger. Scientists knew they had to help.

A black-footed ferret peeks out of a burrow.

A New Hope

At one point, people thought there were no black-footed ferrets left. They thought they were **extinct**. But in 1981, scientists found a small group still alive.

Scientists hoped to keep the ferrets safe. They took them from the wild. They studied the ferrets. They learned what it would take to have more ferrets in the world.

Today, there are programs for **breeding** ferrets. Keepers raise baby ferrets. They help them grow strong.

Dr. JoGayle Howard holds black-footed ferrets that were born in a breeding program.

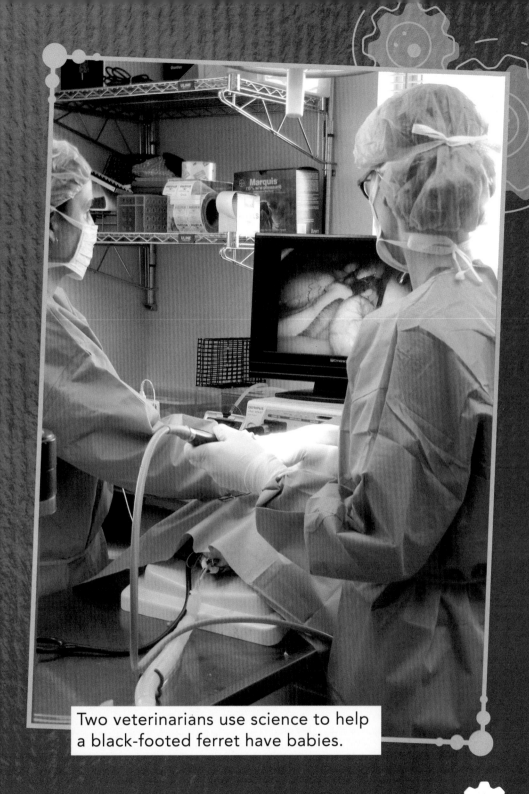

Two veterinarians use science to help a black-footed ferret have babies.

Into the Wild

Some creatures live their whole lives in zoos. They would not be safe in the wild. Other creatures do not stay at zoos for long. This is the case for many black-footed ferrets. When they are old enough, they move to other programs. There, they learn how to survive in the wild.

One thing ferrets are taught is how to hunt prairie dogs. This training helps them hunt in the wild. While they train, ferrets are kept safe from other creatures. This lets them work on their hunting skills.

These black-footed ferrets are too young to be released into the wild.

A black-footed ferret chases a prairie dog.

A park ranger releases a black-footed ferret into the wild.

Ferrets also train to live in burrows. Their bodies are long and thin. Their shape is perfect for tight spaces underground.

During training, workers set up tubes that act as burrows. The tubes show ferrets where to enter. Learning how to live in burrows sets ferrets up for success. In the wild, burrows are where ferrets hunt, sleep, and hide to stay safe.

In the past, ferrets were released without training. They did not do well in the wild. Many died. Ferrets that have been trained are better prepared to survive.

Black-footed ferrets practice entering tubes.

Two black-footed ferrets hide in tubes.

A black-footed ferret peeks out from a burrow in the wild.

23

After ferrets finish training, they have to pass a few tests. First, scientists weigh and measure them. Then, they check their eyes and teeth. Next, they give ferrets medicine. The medicine keeps ferrets safe from diseases. After these tests, ferrets are released into the wild.

Once ferrets are released, scientists check on them. Scientists check ferrets at night. This is when the creatures are awake. Teams shine bright lights where they think ferrets might be. Ferrets' eyes **reflect** light. When teams see the reflection, they write where they saw the ferrets.

This black-footed ferret's eyes are reflecting light.

syringe and microchips

Keeping Track

Scientists want to keep track of ferrets in the wild. So, scientists put small discs called microchips in ferrets. Then, they put microchip readers in the wild. The readers track the ferrets. They tell scientists which ferrets passed by and at what times.

Habitat Sweet Habitat

Zoos help many species survive. Breeding programs help too. Black-footed ferrets were once thought to be extinct. Today, there are hundreds of them. They are making a comeback!

Keepers help animals. They keep them healthy and safe. They are able to do all this because they have great habitats. These habitats make animals feel at home. Creating habitats helps create healthy animals!

A sand cat stretches in its desert habitat.

A southern tamandua climbs in its wooded habitat.

A red-ruffed lemur rests in its rocky habitat.

STEAM CHALLENGE

Define the Problem

A young black-footed ferret is coming to your local zoo. It needs a special home. You have been asked to make a model of its habitat.

 Constraints: Your model must be smaller than 30 centimeters by 30 centimeters (1 foot by 1 foot).

 Criteria: Your model must mimic a ferret's natural habitat. It must have some kind of burrow, a place to sleep, and a place to eat.

Research and Brainstorm

Why should you research an animal before creating an enclosure? What is a black-footed ferret's habitat like in the wild? How do zoos help black-footed ferrets get ready for life in the wild?

Design and Build

Sketch your model. What purpose will each part serve? What materials will work best to build your model? Build the model.

Test and Improve

Show your model to your friends. Does it mimic a black-footed ferret's natural habitat? How can you improve it? Improve your design and try again.

Reflect and Share

Which parts of your model were successful? Where can you improve your model? How might you add technology to your habitat?

Glossary

breeding—keeping and caring for animals to produce more animals

burrows—holes or tunnels in the ground that animals make to live in or to stay safe

enclosure—an area surrounded by something, such as a fence or wall

enrichment—things that encourage animals to use their natural behaviors

extinct—describes a type of animal or plant that has died out completely

habitat—the type of place where an animal or a plant naturally lives and grows

mimic—to look like or appear like something else

natural—existing in nature and not made by humans

reflect—cause light, heat, or sound to bounce off

species—groups of animals or plants that are alike and can produce young together

Index

Career Advice
from Smithsonian

Do you want to work as an animal keeper?

Here are some tips to get you started.

"Be curious about the world around you. Pay attention to details and you will be a great keeper!"—*Ashton Ball, Animal Keeper*

"If you love animals, study to be an animal keeper. You can also volunteer at your local zoo, like I did. You will learn a lot about animals and what they need!" —*Kara Ingraham, Small Mammal House Keeper*